SILLY SCHOOL RIDDLES
AND OTHER CLASSROOM CRACK-UPS

Caroline Anne Levine
Illustrated by Lynn Munsinger

Albert Whitman & Company, Niles, Illinois

Library of Congress Cataloging in Publication Data

Levine, Caroline Anne.
  Silly school riddles and other classroom crack-ups.

  Summary: A collection of over ninety riddles about
school subjects, teachers, tests, and students.
    1. Education—Anecdotes, facetiae, satire, etc.
  2. Wit and humor, Juvenile. [Education—Wit and humor.
  2. Schools—Wit and humor. 3. Riddles] I. Munsinger,
Lynn, ill. II. Title.
PN6231.S3L4 1984   370'.207   84-17300
ISBN 0-8075-7359-0 (lib. bdg.)

The text of this book is set in fourteen-point Optima

Text © 1984 by Caroline Anne Levine
Illustrations © 1984 by Lynn Munsinger
Published in 1984 by Albert Whitman & Company, Niles, Illinois
Published simultaneously in Canada by General Publishing, Limited, Toronto
All rights reserved. Printed in the United States of America.
10   9   8   7   6   5   4   3   2   1

For Rod. **C.L.**

For Scott. **L.M.**

School Stars

Why was Little Dracula popular at recess?
He had the bat.
Why was Cinderella popular at recess?
She had the ball.
Why was Michael Jackson popular at recess?
He had the glove.
Why does Mr. T get perfect report cards?
Because he's on the A-Team.
What rock group guards the school?
The Police.

What did Michael Jackson say to the school bully?
Beat it!

What did the school dietitian say to Weird Al Yankovic?
Eat it!

What did the gym teacher say to Olivia Newton-John?
Get physical!

How often did Cyndi Lauper do her homework?
Time after time.

Silly Susie

What did Silly Susie feed the blackboard?

She gave it chalk-o-late.

Why did Silly Susie bring her teacher butter?

Because he always took the roll.

Silly Susie: Dad, the teacher said that I'm like Washington, Lincoln, and Jefferson.

Dad: Fantastic, Susie! In what way?

Silly Susie: They all went down in history, and so did I!

Librarian: Susie, please don't hum while you read.

Silly Susie: Oh, I'm not reading. I'm just humming.

Why did Silly Susie think her teacher was worried about her eyes?

Because every day she asked, "Oh, say, can you see?"

Teacher: Susie, please spell "mouse."

Silly Susie: M-O-U-S.

Teacher: What's at the end?

Silly Susie: A tail.

Arithmetic

Why did the student put a knife and fork near his computer?

Because it flashed a menu on the screen.

Did you hear what happened to the plant in math class?

It grew square roots.

What's the sum of two big ducks, five little ducks, and three medium ducks?

A box of quackers.

How do monsters count to twenty?
They use their fingers.
If you have six Michael Jackson buttons and
    someone asks for one, how many do you have?
Six. Who would give away a Michael Jackson
    button?
Which month has twenty-eight days?
All of them.
If two's company and three's a crowd, what are
    four and five?
Nine.

Five cats were sitting on a fence. One jumped off.
  How many were left?
None. They were all copycats.
How do you divide eleven apples among twenty
  people?
Make applesauce.
Dad: What are you learning in math, Carol?
Carol: Gozinta, Daddy.
Dad: Is that a new computer language?
Carol: It's just gozinta. Like, two gozinta eight
  twice; eight gozinta sixteen twice.

What Roman numeral climbs the wall?
IV (ivy).

What did one math book say to the other?
Boy, do I have problems!

How many times can you subtract seven from
   seventy-seven?
Once. After that, it's not seventy-seven any more.

What do you get when you add a mommy, a
   daddy, and a baby?
Two and one to carry.

When should teachers wear sunglasses?
When they have bright students.

Aa Bb Cc Gg Hh Ii Mm Nn Oo Ss Tt Uu

What is one bet every first grader learns to make?

Teacher: Jimmy, why are you late for school?
Jimmy: There are seven in our family, and the alarm went off for nine.

TEACHER

The alphabet.

What four letters would scare a burglar?
OICU.

Why didn't the kids like Little Dracula?
Because he was such a pain in the neck.

Lunch

When it's time for lunch, I run a mile around your
  face. What am I?
A smile.
What kind of class monitor is Dracula?
He's the Lunch Count.
In what state do schools serve soft drinks?
Minne-soda.
Where do little cows eat lunch?
In the calf-e-teria.

Teacher: Order, children, order!

Kathy: A cheeseburger, fries, and a coke, please.

What does a ghost take in its lunchbox?

Spook-ghetti and boo-loney sandwiches.

What do you get when you cross an A-student with an Oreo?

One smart cookie!

What do you get when you cross a mystery with a cafeteria?

School lunches.

Test Time

Teacher: You copied from Jeremy's paper, didn't
   you?
Jeff: How can you tell?
Teacher: Because his paper says, "I don't know,"
   and yours says, "Me, neither."
Why did the ditto machine flunk the history test?
The teacher caught it copying.
Josh: Mom, I got a hundred in school today.
Mom: That's terrific! What in?
Josh: Fifty in spelling and fifty in math.
What animal runs around the classroom stealing
   answers?
The cheetah.

What Do You Call . . . ?

What do you call a D and F on your report
  card?
Double trouble.
What do you call an angry principal?
A cross boss.
What do you call a kindergarten class?
A loud crowd.
What do you call teachers at noon?
A lunch bunch.
What do you call someone who steals from the
  school library?
A book crook.
What do you call a chicken's magic marker?
A hen pen.
What do you call your father in the principal's
  office?
A mad dad.

American History

How did the first insects come to the United States?

They came over on the *Mayfly*.

How did the first American barbers arrive?

On clipper ships.

Why did Washington have trouble sleeping?

Because he would never lie.

Where was the Declaration of Independence
  signed?

At the bottom.

What did Ben Franklin say about his lightning
  experiment?
I got the idea in a flash.
In what state did Noah start his voyage?
Ark-ansas.
Which inventors failed to build the airplane?
The Wrong Brothers.
Name the capital of every state in three seconds.
Washington, D.C.

Quick Quizzes

Why did the teacher marry the custodian?
Because he swept her off her feet.

Why do students have such good eyesight?
Because they're pupils.

Why did the teacher throw the ghost out of class?
It was chewing boo-boo gum.

Why did the principal stop calling the bee?
He kept getting a buzzy signal.

Teacher: Rod, name two of the bravest men in American history.

Rod: He-man and Orko.

Teacher: If twelve make a dozen, how many make a million?

Lisa: Oh, maybe Brooke Shields, Matt Dillon, Ricky Schroder . . .

Teacher: Alan, where is the English Channel?

Alan: I don't know. Our TV set doesn't get it.

Teacher: What's an autobiography?

Debbie: I know! It's the life story of a car!

Silly Scott

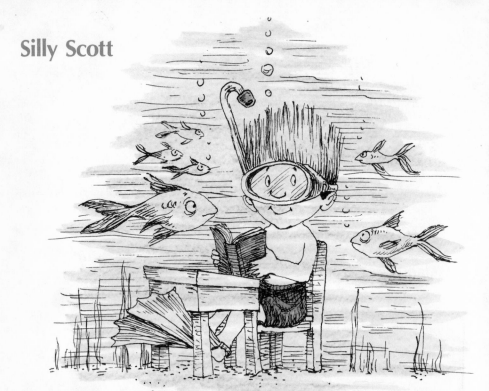

Why did Silly Scott tell his dad his grades were under water?

Because they were below C level.

Teacher: Where is your homework, Scott?

Silly Scott: I made it into an airplane, and it got hijacked.

Why did Silly Scott come to school in a cast?

Because he planned to go break dancing.

Teacher: Scott, please spell "Mississippi."

Silly Scott: Do you mean the river or the state?

Teacher: Can animals solve problems?

Silly Scott: Sure. I asked my dog to subtract ten from ten, and he said nothing.

Why did Silly Scott bake his book report?

The teacher wanted it well done.

Teacher: Why are you scratching yourself, Scott?

Silly Scott: No one else knows where it itches.

What did Silly Scott do when his puppy chewed up his dictionary?

He took the words right out of his mouth.

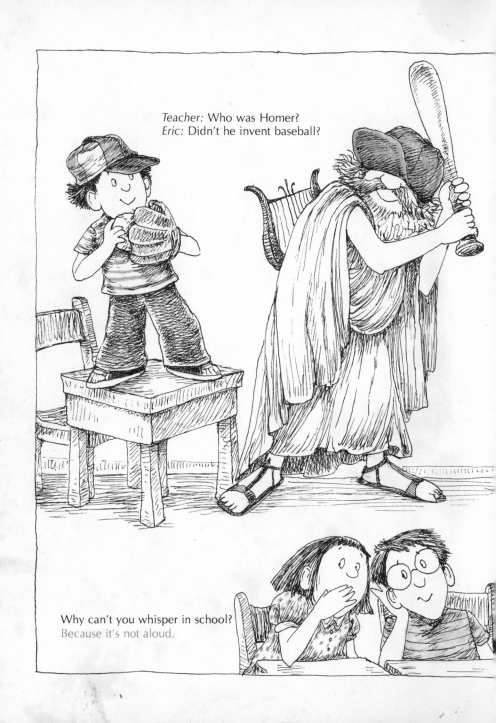

Teacher: Who was Homer?
Eric: Didn't he invent baseball?

Why can't you whisper in school?
Because it's not aloud.

Why was George Washington buried
at Mount Vernon?
Because he was dead.

What's the longest entry in the dictionary?
Post office—it has thousands of letters.

Why did the teacher take her broken
fingernail to the cabinet?
She wanted to file it.

Knock Knocks

Knock, knock.
Who's there?
Ben.
Ben who?
Ben over and get the note I passed you.

Knock, knock.
Who's there?
Shirley.
Shirley who?
Shirley you didn't forget your homework again!

Knock, knock.
Who's there?
Iowa.
Iowa who?
Iowa dime to the library, Mom.

Knock, knock.
Who's there?
Disc.
Disc who?
Disc is the program you put into your computer.

Knock, knock.
Who's there?
Pizza.
Pizza who?
Pizza pie for lunch, please.

Knock, knock.
Who's there?
Wanda.
Wanda who?
Wanda play with me at recess?

Knock, knock.
Who's there?
Venice.
Venice who?
Venice our bus coming?

Quicker Quizzes

What kind of snake is very good at math?
The adder.
What does a farmer use to count his cattle?
A cowculator.
What do mice love most about school?
Field trips.
What island has six sides?
Cube-a.
Who invented geometry?
Joan of Arc.

Name a few things teachers like about their job.

June, July, and August.

What two subjects were named after kids?

Art and Gym.

What do you call someone who loves school
   lunches?

Very hungry.

What is a witch's favorite exam?

A spelling test.

What candy do you eat on school breaks?

Recess Pieces (Reese's Pieces).

What movies get bad grades?

3-D.

What word can you say quicker by adding a
  syllable?

Quick.

What is a cat's best subject?

Meow-sic.

Susie: Did you hear about the boy who took his
dog to school, day after day, until finally the
principal separated them?

Scott: No. What happened?

Susie: The dog graduated.

Caroline Anne Levine lives in Washington, D.C., with her husband, daughter, two miniature dachshunds, and a stuffed animal collection. Her family loves to play practical jokes on her. Once they put a huge watermelon in her garden two days after they watched her plant watermelon seed. She gets back at them by remembering and creating hundreds of jokes and riddles. This is her first book for Albert Whitman.

Lynn Munsinger has illustrated many books for children, including five Albert Whitman picture books: *A Pet for Duck and Bear, Duck Goes Fishing,* and *Bear and Duck on the Run,* all by Judy Delton; *This Little Pig Had a Riddle,* by Richard Latta; and *My Mother Never Listens to Me,* by Marjorie Weinman Sharmat. Lynn lives with her husband in Arlington, Massachusetts.